Newham
in old picture postcards volume 2

by Stephen Pewsey

European Library ZALTBOMMEL/THE NETHERLANDS

Cover picture:
Stratford Broadway in 1915. A
No. 10 London General omnibus,
bound for the Elephant and Castle,
threads its way through heavy
traffic and turns past the Gurney
Monument.

BACK IN TIME

GB ISBN 90 288 6224 2 / CIP
© 1996 European Library – Zaltbommel/The Netherlands

Introduction

It was a great pleasure to be asked to write a second volume covering Newham in this *old picture postcards* series. East and West Ham had a combined population not far short of half a million between the wars, and the richness of this human heritage is here celebrated again in photographic views and postcards. As in the previous volume, these pictures are themed into broad categories: churches, houses and public houses, people, industry, social life, streets and views, transport, and war.

Since the first volume of *Newham in old picture postcards* was published in 1990, exciting archaeological discoveries have been made which shed some light on how people lived in the Newham area in prehistoric times. A Bronze Age timber trackway, about 3,000 years old, was found in Beckton, which can be linked with other finds in the low-lying Thames-side marshes to show that there was a thriving community in the area then, with fishing or religious ceremonies taking place at the water's edge. Meanwhile in Stratford, excavations in advance of the Jubilee Line have revealed Iron Age (500 BC - 0 AD) ritual activity, including the ceremonial burial of a horse. These excavations should in due course also help in understanding the layout of Stratford Langthorne Abbey, which has lain under railway lines for over a century.

It is hoped that this volume will be of interest not just to the people who now live in Newham, but also to the descendants of those many families which moved further afield – particularly after the last war – who may be interested to see the kind of place in which their forbears lived. Older residents still recall streets and scenes now changed out of all recognition: the naphtha flares of the late-night stalls at Angel Lane Market; the good-humoured crowds, up to 40,000 strong, pouring down Prince Regent Lane to watch the speedway at West Ham Stadium in Custom House; variety shows at the Bandstand in Central Park. Since the creation of Newham in 1965, the old boroughs of East and West Ham have been transformed. Many familiar shops and buildings, even a whole lifestyle, may have vanished but, as this book shows, they have not been forgotten.

Acknowledgements
I would like to thank London Borough of Newham for kind permission to use photographs Nos. 3, 12, 15, 54 and 66; Miss Lilian Cameron for No. 24; Walter Scott for No. 40; and Crofton Osmotherley for No. 76. All other images are from the author's own postcard collection or the Eclipse Archive. Thanks are also due to Brian Page for his assistance, and to my wife Paulette for her help and patience.

This book is dedicated to Derek Calder, President of the Newham History Society.

1   All Saints' Church West Ham.

The 74 foot high tower guarding the quiet church-yard has a peal of ten bells. The church has been much altered since Gilbert de Mont-fitchet, the lord of the manor, had it built about 1180, but inside, the walls are still lined with monuments of the many distinguished past residents of West Ham. These include two Lord Mayors of London, Sir Thomas Foot (Lord Mayor in 1649), and Sir John Pelly (Lord Mayor in 1684). The ornate reredos is a reminder of extensive Victorian altera-tions; it was designed by the famous architect Sir George Gilbert Scott, who was also responsible for the Albert Me-morial.

2   St. Mary Magdalene Church East Ham.

This squat, solid church was built by Norman hands from ragstone brought across the Thames from Kent. To this stone they added good Essex flint, and much Roman tile from a settlement so far known only from its burial ground, discovered in 1863 in nearby Roman Road.

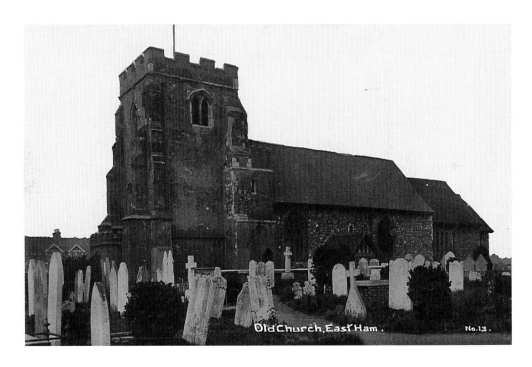

Old Church, East Ham.   No. 13.

3 Apse of St. Mary Magdalene Church.

Two workmen pause for the camera, posed before the lovely semi-circular apse of East Ham's parish church. Uniquely, St. Mary's apse retains its Norman roof timbers intact. Note the blocked door behind them. This was built in the 13th century to provide convenient access for the priest. On the other side of the church, a tiny cell was built into the thickness of the chancel wall, where a hermit lived. A hatch allowed him to see services take place and receive communion.

4 St. Mary's, Plaistow.

As the population of West Ham grew, a new church was required, and St. Mary's was built in 1830. It became a separate parish in 1844, and the original church was rebuilt in an altogether more solid Victorian style. One of the most energetic figures associated with this church was Thomas Given-Wilson, vicar from 1884 until 1914. He raised vast sums of money through worldwide appeals for the poor of Plaistow, creating an elaborate system of social support in the parish; this included a children's hospital, two convalescent homes in Southend-on-Sea and a team of visiting nurses. The church was rebuilt again 1977-1981.

Plaistow   Interior of St. Mary's Church

5   Emmanuel Church.

Two youths prop up a lamp-post in front of this great Victorian double barn of a church. First built in 1852, it was designed by Sir George Gilbert Scott, and the north aisle was enlarged to its present dimensions in 1890.

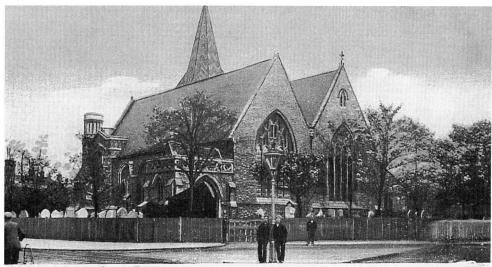

Emanuel Curch, Forest Gate.

The ,,IXL" Series.

6   St. Stephen's, Upton Park.

Another vast Victorian edifice, seen here in a postcard view about 1908. St. Stephen's, first opened in 1887 and completed in 1894, could seat over a thousand and was claimed as the largest church in the diocese. The first vicar was W.G. Trousdale, commemorated today in a Beckton street name (though misspelt Truesdale). The church, which stood on the East Ham side of Green Street, was always strongly associated with High Church rituals. Bombed in 1940, it was demolished in 1954, its site marked by a modern parade of shops.

7 St. Michael's Church, Romford Road.

This postcard view of 1916 shows the church, standing on the corner of Toronto Road. Recently rebuilt, the original church, which itself replaced an iron building, was red-brick Victorian Perpendicular in style. The message on the back of the postcard comments: 'This is a lovely church, but very high. They have a most lovely organ and players.'

ST. MICHAELS CHURCH.

8   St. Francis' Roman Catholic Church, Stratford.

There has always been a strong Catholic presence in Stratford, which was the first Catholic parish in Essex, traditionally established in 1770. Founded in 1868 after vigorous fund-raising efforts by the rector, James McQuoin, the church was at first known as St. Vincent de Paul, after an earlier church of that name which stood in Stratford High Street near the Channelsea Bridge. The name was changed to St. Francis in 1873, after it was taken over by Franciscan friars. The bodies of five nuns laid out here after drowning in 1875 in the Thames Estuary on board the *Deutschland*, inspired poet Gerard Manley Hopkins, himself born in Stratford, to write one of his most famous poems, *The Wreck of the Deutschland*.

S. Francis Church, London E.15 General View.

9 St. Antony's Roman Catholic Church, Forest Gate.

This Pugin-designed church was completed in 1891, together with a friary and school, in Khedive Road, later renamed St. Antony's Road. The land for the church had originally been purchased when the Upton House estate, owned by Lord Lister, was broken up in 1882. A 'chapel school' set up on that land in 1884 was the first Catholic house of studies in England since the Reformation. The church itself long boasted of the largest Catholic congregation in the metropolitan area.

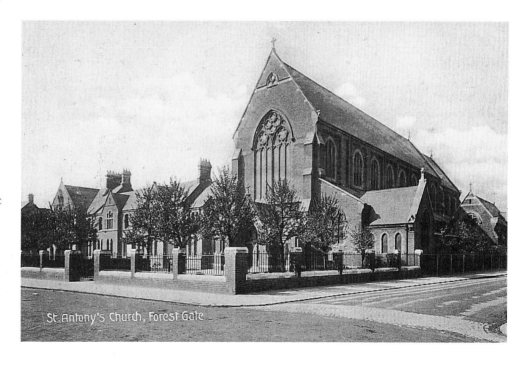

St. Antony's Church, Forest Gate

**10   Brickfields Church,
West Ham.**

This is the oldest nonconformist church in Newham,
with origins dating back to
1662, when a Congregational
chapel was founded in Salway
Place. A new chapel in what is
now Welfare Road was
opened in 1776, and this
view shows the simple in-
terior.

11   New Beckton Baptist Church.

This iron church, affectionately known as 'The Old Green Chapel', was built in Beaconsfield Street in 1888, and served the isolated little community of Cyprus (also known as New Beckton), near Beckton Gasworks. The building was destroyed in an arson attack in 1978, but the brass altar cross was plucked from the flames and now does service in the new ecumenical church of St. Mark in Tollgate Road.

12   Green Street House.

Having concluded our tour of some of Newham's many historic churches, we now take a look at secular buildings. We begin with this 1904 photograph of Green Street House, which stood very close to the present West Ham United football ground. This building, probably built by Giles Breame in the early 16th century, has long been associated with Anne Boleyn, and by tradition Henry VIII courted her here. While not impossible, the tradition is unlikely; tales of tunnels linking the house to the *Old Spotted Dog* or other buildings are certainly untrue, however.

13   Boleyn Castle, about 1900.

One of the most unusual architectural features of Green Street House was this brick tower, nicknamed Boleyn Castle, overlooking the road. The house was, from 1869, associated with Cardinal Manning, who bought it for use as a Roman Catholic reformatory school, and later as a church and school. The tower survived until 1955.

14   The Old Dispensary, Romford Road.

This is one of the oldest timber buildings in West Ham, and has foundations older still; it lies directly over the Roman road from London to Colchester. Built between 1690 and 1720, it was used from 1861 until 1879 as the West Ham, Stratford and South Essex Dispensary, which had been founded by West Ham's Medical Superintendent Dr. William Elliot. Later it was used by William Webb, builder and shopfitter, and more recently it was used as offices by the Passmore Edwards Museum.

15   The *Swan*, Stratford Broadway.

This rare photograph shows the well-known Stratford tavern before the building of the Town Hall in 1869. It is an 18th century structure, though an inn of that name existed at least as early as 1631. In the later 19th century a new façade was added to the ground floor, but the wide stretch of road outside continued to serve as an omnibus and tram terminus well into the 20th century. The pub was rebuilt in about 1925.

16   The *Green Man*, Plashet Grove.

This pub, at the junction of Plashet Grove and Katherine Road, was built in the mid-19th century. Unlike the busy junction of today, the roads in this Edwardian scene are deserted. Note the tramlines in the road; in 1901 East Ham had been the first local authority in the metropolitan area to start its own electric tramway service.

PLASHET GROVE, EAST HAM.

**17   The *White Horse*, High
Street South, East Ham.**

This is the old *White Horse* inn,
demolished in 1905, which
stood at what is now the bus
turning point at the junction
with Rancliffe Road. This road
can be seen on the left, and
tramlines in High Street South
are also visible.

East Ham — The Old "White Horse"

18 *Gallions Hotel*, Beckton.

This splendid Victorian pile was built in 1883 as a terminus hotel beside the Royal Docks. Rudyard Kipling stayed there on his last night in England before he sailed to India, and mentioned it in his tale *The Light that Failed*. The building has recently been restored after a period of dereliction.

19 The *Ferndale*, Cyprus.

This pub was built in about 1881 on the corner of the Cyprus estate, named in honour of the British capture of Cyprus in 1878. Though the Cyprus estate was comprehensively redeveloped in the 1980s, the pub remained.

20   Lord Bethell.

Many famous people have origins in East and West Ham, from comedian Stanley Holloway (1861-1982), to prison reformer Elizabeth Fry (1780-1845). John Henry Bethell (1861-1945), later first Baron Bethell of Romford, however, has a special relationship with East Ham, as he was more or less the founding father of modern East Ham. It was his enthusiasm for the town's development that ensured the building of the Town Hall in 1903, and secured the town's status, first as municipal borough in 1904, then county borough in 1915. His energy was boundless; he also served as a councillor in West Ham, and was M.P. for Romford from 1906 until 1918 and for East Ham from 1918 until 1922, when he was ennobled to the House of Lords.

21   Alfred Stokes.

As well as serving as an East Ham councillor, including a term as mayor in 1921-1922, Alfred Stokes was East Ham's best-known historian. His book *East Ham from Village to County Borough*, published in 1933, remains the best general survey of the area and is full of homely anecdotes.

22 'Bombardier' Billy Wells.

East and West Ham have produced many noted boxers, and one of the greatest was Billy Wells, who lived in Forest Gate. He started his pugilistic career while serving in the army in India, hence his nickname. A Lonsdale Belt holder, he was also world heavyweight champion, one of the last Englishmen to hold that title, and British and Empire heavyweight champion from 1911 to 1919.

23 William Young.

The poverty-stricken areas of Plaistow and Dockland gave plenty of opportunity for urban mission, and literally dozens of small chapels were erected by the various denominations amidst the densely-packed terraces of these areas. Many were short-lived, as although East and West Ham churchgoers were strongly nonconformist, only a minority of the total population actually went to church. The Congregational Church had mission chapels in West Silvertown and Prince Regent Lane, with the main church at Victoria Dock Road. Pastor William Young was Superintendent of the Mission in 1919; shortly afterwards it was taken over by the Shaftesbury Society.

PASTOR WILLIAM YOUNG,
Superintendent South West Ham Congregational Mission.

24   The Reid Family of East Ham.

L.R. Thomas Reid Senior, Thomas Reid Junior, William Reid and John Reid. The Reids typify the enterprising spirit of expanding East and West Ham in the Victorian era. The family originated in Kingston-on-Spey, Morayshire. Thomas Reid Senior was apprenticed at the Thames Iron Works, as were his sons, and he eventually rose to leading carpenter; the sons became ship's joiners, though John Reid also worked as a missionary in Africa. While in what is now Botswana, he was mauled by a leopard which tore his eyelid off! As East Ham expanded, the sons later became house-builders, and built many houses still standing, including some in Central Park Road.

25 St. John's Ambulance Brigade, East Ham.

This photograph shows the worthy ladies of the Nursing Division in 1905. The Brigade's East Ham branch had been founded in 1895.

26 West Ham Park Board School.

More usually known as Park School, the school was opened in Eleanor Road in 1889. Here we see a mixed class sitting to attention.

27   The Royal Docks.

This aerial view of the King George V and Royal Albert Docks shows the docks lined with ships unloading cargo from all over the world. The Royal Docks were the hub of Empire and in their heyday were the busiest in the world. The Royal Victoria Dock had been opened in 1855, 74 acres in extent, and was the first dock to be connected to the rail network. The Royal Albert Dock, 68 acres, was opened in 1880, while the King George V Dock, 65 acres, completed the system in 1921.

28   Royal Albert Dock Basin.

This busy scene shows shipping, goods awaiting distribution in sheds and wagons at the entrance gates. The Royal Albert Dock had its own complex railway system, to ensure the quickest possible transshipment of goods from dock to destination.

29 Beckton Gasworks.

This is a general view of what was once the largest town gas production plant in the world. Local historian Katherine Fry described the scene thus in 1888: 'Midway between East Ham and Woolwich, the electric tramcar halts at the Beckton Road from the entry of which a long wooden barrier has been flung back to admit the vehicles that are continually passing in and out of the Company's domain. As you go forward, on your left are vast heaps of steaming sludge stretching away like a glimpse of chaos, and farther away to the right rise mastheads, looped derricks, coloured funnels and the mazy tackle of great ships. Between these two, nine miles from Charing Cross and amid the dreary Essex flats, lie the famous Beckton Works of the Gas, Light and Coke Company.'

30   Stokers in the retort house, Beckton Gasworks.

Seen here in the 1890s, this work demanded great physical strength and stamina. Toiling in the heat and filth predisposed the workmen to demand better conditions, and in 1889 Will Thorne founded the Gas Workers' Union, the forerunner of the modern super-union the GMB.

31 Beckton Sewage Works.

Beckton not only boasted the largest gasworks in the world, but also the largest sewage works in Europe. London's Outfall Sewer System was originally designed by Sir Joseph Bazalgette, to remove the capital's effluent to a safe distance, then discharge it into the Thames. On the northern bank, the sewage was discharged at Beckton, at the estuary of Barking Creek. At first the sewage was released untreated, but the first Sewage Treatment Works was built in 1890, eventually expanding in the 1960s to the large site seen in this aerial photograph. Barking Creek lies to the right.

32   Abbey Mills Pumping Station.

Opened in 1868, this was Bazalgette's architectural masterpiece, a 'temple of effluvium', the interior designed in Venetian gothic style, but constructed of cast iron. Four great beam engines were employed to pump London's sewage on its way to the Thames. Any one of the engines was capable of pumping a million gallons of sewage per hour through the 10 ft cast-iron sewer!

33 West Ham Pumping Station.

Ironically, West Ham had no access to the Outfall Sewer, which was designed for London's sewage; West Ham lay over the border in Essex. Sewage disposal was therefore an unpleasant but ever-present problem for the West Ham corporation, and the matter was not resolved until 1893, when agreement was reached for connection to the Outfall Sewer. First though, a pumping station had to be built to transfer the sewage into the main system, and this was West Ham Pumping Station, opened in 1901 in Ab-bey Road. This photograph is a fine interior view of the building, which still stands.

34   H.M.S. *Warrior*.

West Ham once had a proud shipbuilding tradition. The firm of C.J. Mare & Co was founded in Bow Creek in 1846, and renamed Thames Ironworks in 1856. The *Warrior*, built in 1860, was the first of a new generation of iron-clad battleships, and at the time was the biggest and fastest warship afloat. After many years of neglect, the *Warrior* has now been restored and is preserved at Portsmouth. The Thames Ironworks went on to build many other warships, but closed in 1912 in the face of competition from the shipyards of Tyneside and Wearside. One lasting legacy was, however, the works football team, the 'Irons', which survives and thrives today in the form of West Ham United, founded in 1900 from an amalgamation of several teams including the Thames Ironworks team.

35 The House Mill, Abbey Mills.

So named from the fact that they once belonged to Stratford Langthorne Abbey, only two of the 'Three Mills' survive. The House Mill dates from 1776 and was built by one Daniel Bisson, probably a Huguenot, and is the largest surviving tidal watermill in the country. To the right of the mill stands the miller's house, damaged by wartime bombing, but restored in 1995 as a visitor centre. The House Mill itself is undergoing longterm restoration.

36   The Clock Mill, Abbey Mills.

Built in 1817, this mill, with its distinctive 'oast-house' drying kiln, has long been associated with gin-distilling. This seems to have been founded by another Huguenot, Peter Lefevre, in the 18th century. Before that, earlier mills on the site were used for corn-milling and gunpowder-milling.

37 Windmill at Stratford.

Together with the watermills, there were once also a large number of windmills near the Lea and the Bow Back Rivers. Medieval Stratford had a highly-developed economy based on these mills. Huge quantities of corn were ground in the ceaseless querns, and the flour was then used to make bread, the ovens being fired with brush-wood and faggots from near-by Epping Forest. Stratford bread was then delivered to London, where it was well known; Bakers Row recalls the trade.

38   Larkins Confectioners, High Street North, East Ham.

Both East Ham and Stratford have in their time been shopping centres, attracting visitors from many smaller surrounding towns. One of the best-known small traders was Harry Larkin, born in 1880, who developed a network of confectionery and greengrocery shops across East and West Ham, and eventually stretching out across much of south Essex. This photograph shows Daisy Larkin and Dolly Miller standing outside their High Street shop in 1930.

39   Burton's, High Street North, East Ham.

Montague Burton arrived in Britain from Lithuania in 1900, and set up his first shop in Chesterfield, which soon expanded to a nation-wide chain of stores, easily recognisable from their distinctive façades. Here the East Ham branch proclaims itself the 'Palace of Fashion.'

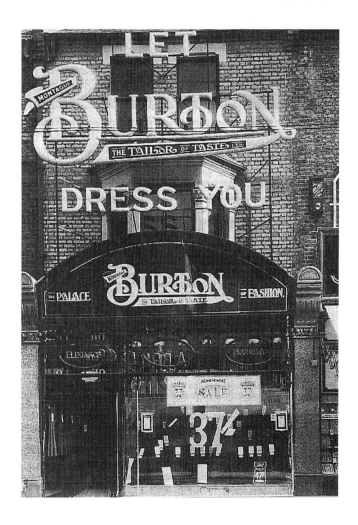

40 The Greengate Cinema.

The reason for this huge gathering of children about 1920 is unknown, but it is a splendid photograph of the Greengate Cinema. Standing next to the pub of the same name, it first opened in about 1912, and later changed its name to the Rio. Here the silent film *Kilties Three*, a patriotic war adventure, is being shown. Going to the cinema was one of the most popular inter-war leisure activities, and there were at least nineteen picture-palaces in West Ham alone.

41   Passmore Edwards Museum.

On an altogether higher cultural plane was the Passmore Edwards Museum, opened in 1900 as the Essex Museum and largely devoted to natural history. This unusual interior view shows both the main gallery on the ground floor and the balcony gallery in the rotunda. The Museum was closed by Newham Council in 1994.

42 Works outing by charabanc.

This delightful postcard shows a group of workmen in their Sunday best on an outing from the Leathercloth Co., which had a large factory in Abbey Road. The picture, which dates from the 1920s, was taken outside the *Spread Eagle* pub in Manor Road. Southend-on-Sea was a particularly popular destination for such outings, particularly after the completion of the Arterial Road (A127) in 1925.

43 West Ham Park.

With a combined population reaching a peak of over 400,000 in 1921, East and West Ham cherished the little open space that remained in the boroughs, and the parks were valuable 'green lungs'. One of the largest of these is West Ham Park, acquired by the City of London, and opened to the public on 20th July 1874. This postcard dates from 1909.

WEST HAM PARK, STRATFORD, E.

44   The Gardens, West Ham Park.

The park originally formed the grounds of Ham House, home of the philanthropic Quaker banking family the Gurneys. Ham House was demolished in 1872, and the site was marked with a large cairn of stones (into which was incorporated a drinking fountain), seen here in this view. The presence of the cannon behind the cairn is unexplained, but there was an army depot nearby at a large house called The Cedars, in Portway.

45   The Round Seat, West Ham Park.

In this charming Edwardian scene, a policeman rests his tired frame at the end of a long beat. The marvellous array of trees, plants and shrubs in the park is living testimony to the work of Dr. John Fothergill, owner of Ham House before the Gurneys. He bought the estate in 1762 and imported rare and exotic plants from around the globe, turning the grounds into a world-famous botanical garden, second only to Kew.

THE ROUND SEAT, WEST HAM PARK.

East Ham's founding civic father, John (later Lord) Bethell, recognised that with rapid building development, open land for use as parks and recreation grounds had to be secured as quickly as possible before bricks and mortar covered the area. Plashet Park, originally the grounds of Wood House, was acquired in 1889 and opened in 1891, East Ham's first municipal park.

47   New Beckton Park.

This 13-acre park off Manor
Way was opened in 1901 for
the benefit of residents of
Savage Gardens. There were
cricket and football pitches as
well as the ornamental lake
and bandstand seen in this
photograph.

48   Portway, West Ham.

This postcard, dating from about 1907, introduces a selection of views of the streets of East and West Ham. A tram is trundling towards Stratford, while on the left pedestrians are passing West Ham Park. The gatehouse by the tram has been demolished.

49   High Street North, East Ham.

The ornate terracotta façade of the shopping parade has changed little since this post-card was issued about 1906. The junction with Plashet Grove is on the left.

50 Barking Road.

Here is a lively scene outside the *Boleyn* tavern in 1915. The streets are crowded with shoppers, and there is a long queue for the bus to Barking. On the other side of the road, beyond the shopping parade, the tower of the Empire Kinema can be seen. This was later known simply as the Empire; opened in 1914, it closed in 1936 and was later demolished.

Barking Road, East Ham.

51   Romford Road.

St. John's Church lies directly
in front; built in 1834 on the
remnants of Stratford Green,
the church was at first a cha-
pel-of-ease, gaining parish
status a decade later. The roads
seem remarkably deserted in
this view!

Romford Road, Stratford.

The „IXL" Series.

52 Chestnut Avenue, Forest Gate.

A quiet suburban street in the residential area of Forest Gate, about 1910. The street took its name from a magnificent avenue of chestnut trees, which once lined the road from Romford Road and across Wanstead Flats to Wanstead House.

Chestnut Avenue, Forest Gate.

53   Green Street.

This view shows the hustle and bustle which has characterised Green Street for many years. Known as Grene Lane in 1527, the road is of great antiquity, now best known as the venue for a bustling Asian market. In this view, a No. 40 bus bound for Camberwell High Road is being followed by a No. 685 trolleybus, on its way to Canning Town station from the *Crooked Billet*, Walthamstow.

GREEN STREET, EAST HAM.

E.H.14

54   Woodgrange Road.

This is Forest Gate's main shopping centre; in this turn-of-the-century view, a two-wheeled cart speeds past the rows of shops, with the spire of Forest Gate Methodist Church prominent on the left. Forest Gate Station, on the Great Eastern line to Southend-on-Sea, lies in the distance.

55   Leytonstone Road.

This 1909 view shows the range of shops in this area, known as Maryland Point; note the shop in the middle left called 'The Point'. Trinity Presbyterian Church can also be seen.

The *Swan* is prominent in the foreground, but the road is oddly free of traffic; perhaps this view was taken early on a Sunday. On the right, a parade of shops stretches away into the distance, while St. John's Church is out of sight on the left. Note the tramlines curving away to the right on the far side of the *Swan*. Now Tramway Avenue, this road once led straight into the Corporation tramway depot.

57   Romford Road.

A busy scene from 1920; a horse and cart on the left, but approaching us is a motor omnibus, the No. 25A bound for Victoria Station. On the left, the West Ham Technical Institute and Central Library (opened 1898), with the shallow dome of the Pass-more Edwards Museum (opened 1900) beyond. The technical institute is now a campus of the University of 'East London.'

58　High Street North, East Ham.

In this 1903 postcard, East Ham Tramways Car No. 20, built in 1901, is approaching East Ham station on its way to the Royal Albert Dock terminus.

59 Plashet Grove.

By way of contrast, an open-top tram passes Plashet Library with Upton Park on its destination board. The library, East Ham's first purpose-built library, was opened in 1899, following a donation of £4,000 by philanthropist Passmore Edwards.

PLASHET GROVE.

60 Savage Gardens, Beckton.

East Ham pioneered the building of council housing – then known as artisans' dwellings – and this photograph shows the first, Savage Gardens, opened in February 1901. Named after Councillor John Savage, these maisonettes were by the standards of the day very spacious and well appointed.

61 Winsor Terrace, Beckton.

This isolated parade of houses was built in 1870 to house workers from the nearby Beckton Gasworks; the larger houses were for supervisory staff. The name is taken from Frederic Winsor, founder of the Gas Light & Coke Company in 1809 and inventor of town gas.

62 Stratford Broadway.

A policeman strolls past the *Coach and Horses* in this 1912 view, with the dome of Stratford Town Hall in the distance beyond St. John's Church. Three great stores, Boardman's, J.R. Roberts and the Co-op, dominated the Stratford shopping scene, but the market in Angel Lane attracted visitors from miles around.

THE BROADWAY, STRATFORD.

63 Aerial view of Stratford, 1934.

Many important buildings can be seen in this unusual view. St. John's Church dominates the town centre. At the bottom right, Stratford Town Hall can be seen, and beyond it the zig-zag roofs of the tram depot. Romford Road stretches away towards the top right of the postcard, while in The Grove the colonnade and classical portico of the Central Baptist Church are visible at the top left.

The free ferry from North Woolwich to Woolwich was an important component in the local transport system, to say nothing of providing hours of entertainment for small boys with nothing but to do but travel back and forth across the narrow stretch of water. The 1910 view shows *Duncan*, one of the original paddle steamers which worked the route from 1899 to the First World War.

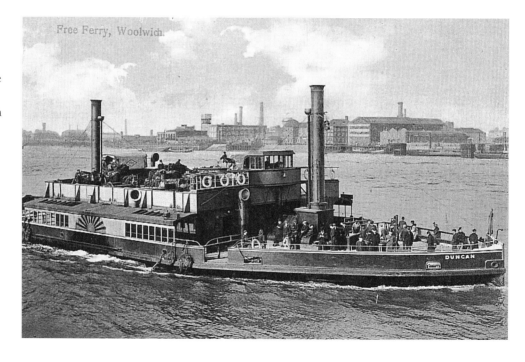

65 Bascule Bridge, Beckton.

This curious looking contraption was built in 1903 as part of the Barking Urban District Council tramway from Barking to Beckton. Seen here about 1920, the bridge was necessary to allow shipping access to Barking's Town Quay. The tramway was popular with workers at Beckton Gasworks, many of whom lived in Barking, but was closed and replaced by a bus service in 1929.

Car No. 42 pauses en route to
Plaistow about 1904, the year
West Ham Corporation
opened its first electric tramway.

67 Tram Terminus, Wanstead Flats.

West Ham's Car No. 65 stands at the Woodford Road terminus about 1904. The houses in Capel Road in the distance overlook the flats, where benches have been laid out for the benefit of visitors.

Tram Terminus, Wanstead Flats, Forest Gate. E.

68 Locomotive Works, Stratford Railway Works.

First established in 1839, the railway works grew to become a vast enterprise, employing thousands in jobs as diverse as locomotive construction and timetable printing. This early photograph dates from 1864 and shows the locomotive assembly shed, where at least half a dozen locos are under construction.

69   Carriage Works, Stratford Railway Works.

In the carriage works meanwhile, carriages were being widened to accommodate six rather than four abreast.

Opened in 1841 as part of the Eastern Counties (later Great Eastern) Railway line to Romford, this is one of the more ornate stations on the line. The cupola has recently been restored after years of neglect. The availability of workmen's tickets on railway lines east of London played an important role in the rapid development of both West and East Ham as well as suburbs further from London.

Forest Gate Station.

71   Royal Albert Dock Locomotive.

Loco No. 6 was one of the original engines used on the Royal Albert Dock Passenger Line, which ran from Custom House to Gallions along the north side of the Royal Albert Dock. The line opened in 1880, and this loco was one of three originally purchased from the LNWR, where it served as No. 250, *John o'Gaunt*. The service ran until 1909, when it was taken over by the Port of London authority; the line was badly damaged in the Blitz and never reopened.

72   Peace Tea, Ethel Road, West Ham, 1919.

More than 100,000 West Ham men served in the armed forces during the First World War and many hundreds did not return home; the out-patients department at Queen Mary's Hospital in Stratford formed West Ham's official war memorial. When peace broke out in 1918, there were spontaneous celebrations, followed by further festivities after the Versailles peace conference of 1919. Here we see the people of Ethel Road in Custom House gathered for their peace tea, while a stout constable looks on.

73 German bomber raid over Beckton, 1940.

The 'Phoney War' came to an abrupt end on 7th September 1940, the first day of the Blitz, and recalled in Newham as 'Black Saturday'. The docks and industries in the south of the borough were particularly hard hit and the fires could be seen for many miles around. Here we see Luftwaffe bombers directly over Beckton and the docks. The oval of West Ham Stadium, Custom House, can be seen in the middle of the frame, to the left of Beckton Road (now Tollgate Road).

74   Firefighting during the blitz, Beckton Gasworks.

Beckton Gasworks was repeatedly hit in the period from September to December 1940, but employees made heroic efforts to keep gas production going. The Superintendent W. Gordon Adam won a George Medal for risking his life to put out fires in the highly-inflammable By-Products Works. Here a team of firefighters struggles to contain a blaze.

75   Bomb damage in the Blitz, Beckton Gasworks.

Smashed wagons dangle crazily out of the archway, part of the internal overhead railway system within the gasworks.

76 Waste ground near Balaam Street.

After the war, there was a massive job of reconstruction. Nearly a third of all buildings in West Ham were destroyed by bombing or so badly damaged they had to be demolished. Hitler's Blitz had cleared away massive areas of slums, and in some areas like Canning Town, planners could start afresh and build what was practically a new town. In many areas, however, redevelopment was slow, and waste ground lay idle, awaiting action. In this 1949 photograph, a wide stretch of land lies vacant from Balaam Street to Grange Road, with bomb-shattered houses to the right.